MATERIAL
MATTERS

First published and distributed by
viction:workshop ltd.

viction:ary™

viction:workshop ltd.
Unit C, 7/F, Seabright Plaza, 9-23 Shell Street,
North Point, Hong Kong
Url: www.victionary.com
Email: we@victionary.com
▮ @victionworkshop
▮ @victionary_
▮ @victionworkshop

Edited & produced by viction:ary

Creative direction by Victor Cheung
Book design by viction:workshop ltd.

ISBN 978-988-79033-1-4
Printed and bound in China

MATERIAL MATTERS

VOLUME
ONE:

WOOD

CREATIVE
INTERPRETATIONS
OF
COMMON
MATERIALS

Excerpt by John Heskett

'Design: A Very Short Introduction'
Oxford University Press, 2005

"The human capacity to design has remained constant even though its means and methods have altered, in parallel to technological, organisational, and cultural changes. 'The historical evolution of design' argues that design, although a unique and unchanging skill, has manifested itself in different ways throughout time. The diversity of concepts and practices in modern design is explained by the layered nature of the evolution of design. It is difficult to determine exactly when humans began to change their environment to a significant degree, or in other words to design. Whose interest will design serve in the future? How will design cope with challenges of operating in a more globalised space?"

In what is believed to be his most translated book to-date, writer and educator John Heskett posed some pertinent questions about the future as he perused the application, philosophy, and history of design. Besides underlining the importance of humanising technology and offering readers an exciting glimpse into what could be, Heskett also sought to transform perceptions about design by proving how truly inextricable it is from our daily lives. Instead of merely focusing on the complex inventions that demonstrate how far we have come and how much we are truly capable of achieving for the human race, he examined the simplest of everyday objects to remind us how impactful their designs are and will continue to be, no matter how modest they may seem at first glance.

Fast forward to 2019 where the digital behemoth shows no signs of slowing down since it first appeared, steamrolling over every aspect of our existence. As much as passion and dedication remain timeless humanistic qualities that determine one's progress or trajectory in all fields including art and design, technology has not only broken down physical, spiritual, and ideological barriers, but also opened up whole new dimensions for exploration and experimentation. On a granular level, automation and computerised processes have helped us to do more, get better, and go further than we ever have since the Industrial Revolution in the 18th and 19th centuries; affecting the ways with which we create and appreciate all that is around us.

Although demand plays a big part in determining what gets produced, the market today is often flooded with goods and services that people do not actually need but exist simply because technology and unscrupulous sellers have enabled them to. As consumers become trapped in a mindless cycle of wanting and buying, they end up paying the price in more ways than one - all this because they are being sold ideals and empty messages through advertising and marketing, rather than meaning and purpose. Not all is lost, however, as Heskett's observations are slowly but surely proving to be more relevant than they have ever been.

In recent times, there has been a significant increase in the number of maker communities online and offline, thanks in no small part to the rise in hyper-consumerism and its not-too-distant cousin, the 'throw-away culture'. According to a report by the Royal Society of Arts, the maker movement reflects our society's push against significant technological upheaval, with the underlying goal of giving the power back to the people. Rather than let brands have complete control over our mindsets and habits, what we are saying is 'enough is enough' by choosing self-reliance and a sense of agency. Due to buyers who are becoming more discerning about a product's origins and contents, as well as the craftsmanship and artisanal value behind it, independent sellers are finally seeing their integrity, thoughtfulness, and capabilities be recognised and aptly rewarded.

While this does not mean that mass manufacturing will cease to be a part of our world completely, we are excited about this shift in the realm of art and design. Beyond graphics, illustrations, and colour palettes that are obvious to the naked eye, it is time that materials get the spotlight they deserve. Whether it is used as a textured finish or the canvas of creation itself, the power of material lies in its ability to connect creators to their audiences on a deeper level. Visceral and tactile, it allows every creative experience to evoke an emotional response through touch and feel; universal languages that speak to the senses in a truly authentic manner.

Through our MATERIAL MATTERS series, we hope to inspire readers with the infinite possibilities that embracing, enhancing, and transforming common materials allow for by taking a closer look at the elements that we typically ignore around us. From stamping subtle wood grains onto a piece of stationery to generate a striking pattern to transforming a pristine metal sheet into a rusted sculptural masterpiece, we celebrate the extraordinary beauty in the ordinary, as brought to life across a variety of mediums by the artists and designers featured in our books. After all, just as Heskett posited, means and methodologies of art and design may continue to alter, but at the end of the day, the foundation of creativity as a pure expression of the heart and soul will never falter.

Wood has been an essential material to mankind since the beginning of time. Although it may have been used solely for shelter and survival in the beginning, our ancestors eventually found ways to make the most of its unique physical properties and charm beyond laying the foundations of modern civilisation; resulting in its current role as a canvas, component, and source of inspiration for a variety of creative pursuits. Whether it is the warmth and comfort that emanate from its earthy shades or the instant connection that one inadvertently forms with the wilderness and nature upon first laying eyes on its textured surface or grains, wood has a timeless appeal that adds character and underlying strength to any project; making it imperative for us to obtain it in ethical manners and preserve its supply for our future generations to enjoy.

In featuring as many techniques as possible that bring out its best, all the creative work in this book has been curated based on three key categories that cover the interesting and impactful ways with which the artists and designers have utilised, applied, and pushed the limits of the material.

EMBRACE

As a natural material with so much inherent beauty, some of the artists and designers in this book have chosen to honour wood in all its solid, textured, and grainy glory in realising their visions. Whether they used part of a tree trunk as is, assembled different branch varieties, made their own annual ring patterns, or reproduced wooden elements using entirely different materials, they have achieved striking outcomes through subtle levels of creative re-interpretations. From elegant visual identities to elaborate pieces of art, their work is a celebration of wood for all that it already is.

ENHANCE

It is as meaningful for artists and designers to have their messages resonate effectively with their audiences, as it is for them to leave their style or signature on a piece of work. Although wood can convey many stories as it is, enhancing it with different creative skills and techniques such as unique colour treatments and intricate etchings can take it to a whole different level. The dichotomy of its strength and flexibility as well as its absorbent nature, makes it a unique material to manipulate and create exciting outcomes with, as some of the artists and designers in this book have done.

TRANSFORM

Experimentation is a form of creative play that many indulge in to build their skills and discover new styles in the process. Due to its elasticity and the relative ease with which it can be altered, wood has presented some of the artists and designers in this book with many technical and innovative possibilities to explore the creation of optical illusions, one-of-a-kind objects, and even different matter altogether. Besides highlighting the power of the creator's imagination, each featured work also gives prominence to the multidimensional capabilities of a cherished and timeless material.

One of the oldest known techniques in art, wood carving entails using a cutting tool or a chisel and mallet to manually create new forms or enhance an existing object through sculptural ornamentation. Picking the right type of wood is essential for this craft, as an unsuitable one could limit the scope of the carver.

In order to carve wood effectively, the artist or designer should try to follow the grain or the direction in which the wood is the strongest. Although this might not always be possible due to the organic way grains exist (e.g. interlocked, wavy), it is best to place the more intricate parts of the design being carved in the 'line of best fit'. Softwoods like basewood and butternut are popular choices for beginners and good for whittling, whereas hardwoods like maple and oak can be harder to handle but hold a finish well.

For more sculptural work, various gouges can be used for the general shaping process. A gouge is a curved blade that can remove large portions of wood smoothly, in that the harder the type of wood is, the sharper the gouge should be. Although chisels differ from gouges with their flat blades, carvers generally refer to both of them as chisels. Other tools like veiners, fluters, 'v'-tools, or rasps can also be used to make fine lines, deep cuts, and smooth surfaces. Similar to the carving process, it is best to follow the grain when sculpting wood. To finish the final woodwork, one can polish it with sandpaper or seal the surface with natural oils like walnut or linseed oil for protection.

(Source: en.wikipedia.org)

CARVING

COLLAGE

Derived from the French term which means 'to glue', collage is an art form that involves assembling different pieces to create a new whole. Although it was coined by artists Georges Braque and Pablo Picasso at the turn of the 20th century when it was deemed to be a distinctive part of modern art, the technique can actually be traced further back in time. Typically, collages can include anything from magazine or newspaper clippings, ribbons, photos, and portions of text to found objects - all of which are glued onto a single surface.

The wood collage emerged somewhat later than the paper collage, when Kurt Schwitters began experimenting with the technique in the 1920s after being inspired by Braque, who would attach pieces of oak grain-patterned wallpaper onto his charcoal drawings. Further on,

American sculptor Louise Nevelson began pushing the boundaries of her work in the mid-1940s through intense experimentation; assembling her collages with furniture scraps and architectural remnants like railings and mouldings to produce gigantic masterpieces.

Today, wood collages are considerably smaller in scale and usually feature creative combinations of wood pieces or shavings. AFTSTUDIO's Veneer Marquetry project on page 158 showcases the striking outcomes of fusing various graphic and organic wooden shapes. Their abstract works of art lent a breath of fresh air to classic marquetry landscape art in an interesting and impactful way.

(Source: en.wikipedia.org)

Laser-cutting has become one of the more popular techniques employed by artists and designers today in producing intricate and intriguing work. For projects or materials where drag-knife cutters like craft cutters and vinyl cutters are unsuitable, laser cutters function as high-precision machines with narrow laser beams that lead to versatile processes and outcomes. Whether they are used to create unique pieces of jewellery or highly-detailed scrapbooking elements, they allow for more experimentation and shorter idea-to-production times.

A laser cutter uses plug-ins and vector graphics applications to create the foundation for a creative project. Newer machines have a tab-and-slot construction that make them easy to assemble and take apart for further convenience. Although the bigger ones are expensive to own, there is a growing number of more affordable laser cutters in the market that make for highly reliable, credible, and valuable pieces of investment. The best type of wood for laser-cutting are said to be maple, in terms of how much power is required and how 'clean' the cut edges are afterwards.

On page 140, Elisa Strozyk took this technique to the next level by making a whole new material out of wood. In seeking to push the latter's boundaries in form and function, she laser-cut tiles from deconstructed wooden pieces to create Wooden Textiles to reflect their flexible and mobile sculptural possibilities.

(Source: makezine.com)

LASER-CUTTING

ENGRAVING

Developed at the end of the 18th century by Thomas Bewick, wood engraving was a printmaking and letterpress-printing technique that has become the foundation for many modern art and design projects. In the past, an image would be worked into a block of wood and then appled ink to before printing in a method known as relief printing. As time went on, although more people began using a metal plate and the intaglio printing method which is the opposite of relief printing technique-wise, wood engravings survived because of their distinct charm and character.

The endgrain of hardwoods like maple is considered to be the best block or surface for this technique, due to the fact that it can hold a high level of detail and last longer. An endgrain can be obtained by cutting timber across its annual rings. Although laser-engravings are growing in popularity on wood blocks, many people still enjoy engraving by hand.

Today, a wide range of specialised tools can be utilised; depending on the complexity of the design being engraved. The burins that were used during Bewick's time to engrave copper became the base for lozenge gravers. 'V'-shaped gravers, spitstickers, and scorpers in various sizes can hatch, create curvy lines, and define textures respectively. During the process, the wood block is typically sandwiched between the chosen tool and a sandbag that can be rotated and moved underneath to manipulate the results.

(Source: en.wikipedia.org)

Some artists and designers prefer paying homage to a material, rather than use it as their canvas or medium. Whether they seek to push the boundaries of their own imaginations by transforming something beyond recognition or producing optical illusions to intrigue their audiences, there are many reasons for recreating wood out of non-wood objects.

The most common way to do so is by repurposing more malleable materials like fabric and paper to imitate the more solid construct of a wooden element. Other tools like paint can help the artist or designer realistically reproduce its textures and grains or re-interpret natural elements entirely through the use of unexpected colours. Some wood recreations even feature reclaimed or recycled wooden pieces; making them complex yet compelling concepts.

Ultimately, when it comes to creative projects, personal preferences and purpose takes centrestage. For artist Tamara Kostianovsky on page 136, she was inspired by the South American people of the Andes who believe that Mother Earth is embodied by their surrounding mountains to make severed tree stumps out of her late father's clothing. By translating simple yet meaningful everyday items into sculptures that represent the environment and passing of time, she recreated wood in a thoughtful way.

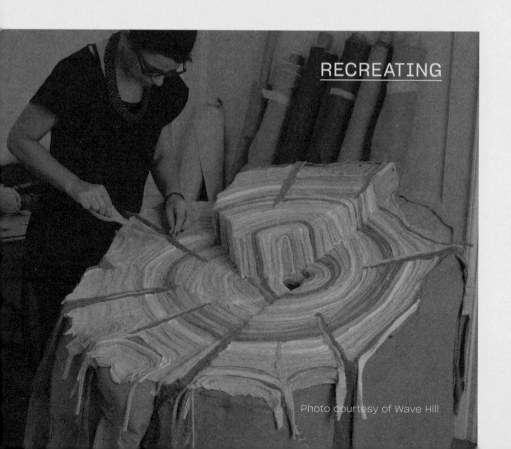

RECREATING

Photo courtesy of Wave Hill

SANDBLASTING

Sandblasting, also known as abrasive blasting, involves forcibly directing a stream of abrasive material against a surface under high pressure. The type of abrasive material used differs according to the surface it is to be directed upon, but sand is typically chosen due to the fine but rough grains of the former, and the relatively softer texture of the latter. Although it is primarily used to remove grit, sandblasting is a quick and efficient process to smoothen, weather, strip, or shape wooden surfaces.

Generally, an industrial sandblasting system consists of the sandblasting cabinet, the air source, the blasting media, and the dust collector. The sandblasting cabinet forms the 'base' that holds the surface being blasted, whereas the air source - usually bottled gas or an air compressor - propels the blasting media or sand. If the project is simpler or on a smaller scale, only a sandblasting pressure pot and sand are needed.

For Dutch designer Lex Pott's collaborative project with New Window on page 78, pieces of wood were sandblasted to reveal the annual rings of a Douglas fir tree that was planted around 1960 and felled in 2013. By covering different portions of their surfaces with rubber stickers during the sandblasting process, objects of various sizes, patterns, and functions were born; lending meaning to project name 'Diptych' which refers to the juxtaposition within each object.

(Sources: en.wikipedia.org, www.princeton.edu)

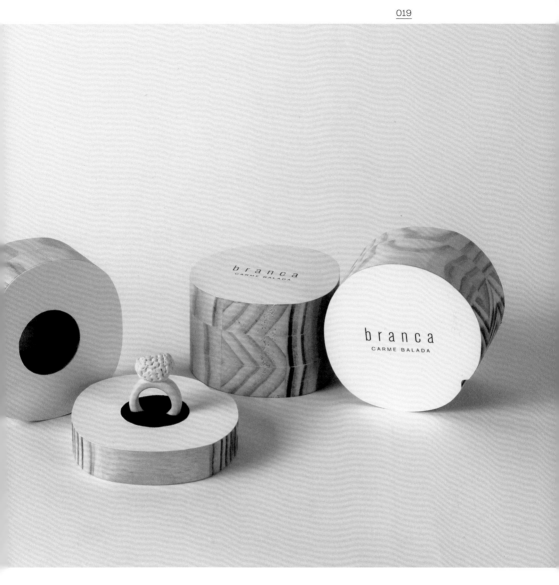

WORK TYPE | Packaging
DESIGN | Elisava Pack, Carine Attar (Graphic), Anna Gené Casellas (Product)

For their master's degree project, Carine Attar and Anna Gené Casellas collaborated on a jewellery box design brief for Carme Balada, a ceramic artist who focuses on fusing the richness and sensibilities of traditional methods with a contemporary style. In analysing and empathising with the artist's philosophy, they sought to reflect the craftsmanship, cultural sensitivity, and tranquility that goes into her work by encapsulating the distinctive characteristics of natural wooden forms.

BRANCA

WORK TYPE | Packaging
DESIGN | Zunder OG
CLIENT | Hermann Knogler

Everything about Zirbn, Hermann Knogler's limited edition Swiss pine liquor, can be encapsulated in eight words: 'aus zirbn, vom zirbn, zum zirbn, in zirbn'. To reflect this reduction in Austrian dialect and encapsulate the inventor-distiller's exquisite craftsmanship, Zunder OG were inspired to keep their packaging design work pure and simple. By bottling the liquor in containers made from Swiss pine wood, they successfully emboded Hermann's spirit of artistry and authenticity.

HERMANN KNOGLER
– ZIRBNLIKÖR

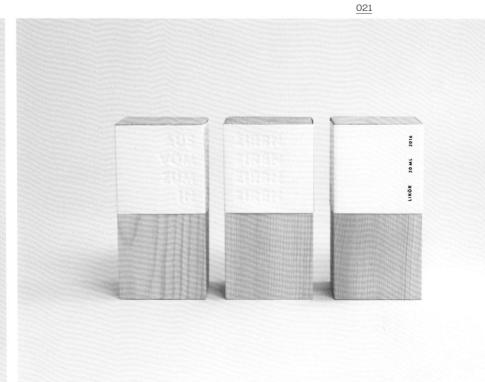

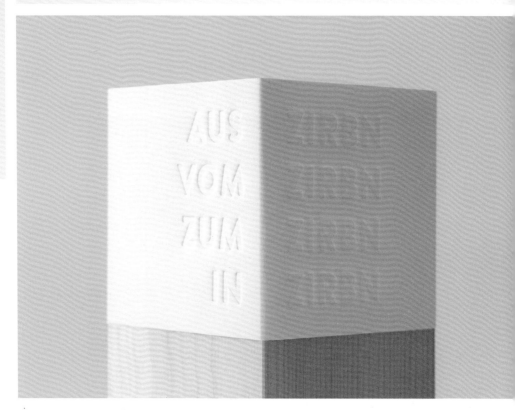

WORK TYPE | Art
ARTWORK | Oksana Drachkovska

From the Virgin Mary's suffering during Jesus's crucifixion to a beggar's plea for a place in Paradise, Stabat Mater is a Roman Catholic hymn that is full of significant religious moments. In bringing its profound ideas to life, Oksana Drachkovska drew upon her research in iconography and book design to create a symbolic visual language. By drawing parallels between layers of culture and sections of wood, she added new meaning to a classical legacy that essentially outlines the history of mankind.

STABAT MATER

What
the
hack
is
future?

Raphael Gielgen
— Vitra

Research/
Trend Scouting

6.10.2016
18.30

Tabakfabrik
Linz

AREA　vitra.　　　area.at

WORK TYPE | Event Collateral
DESIGN | OrtnerSchinko
CLIENT | AREA create identity
PHOTOGRAPHY | Jürgen Grünwald

AREA's lecture series in 2016 with Raphael Gielgen, the head of Vitra's trend research office, was themed 'What the hack is future?', where issues regarding workspace functionalities and their future possibilities were addressed. OrtnerSchinko created an intriguing visual identity based on a revolutionary table system and material called the Vitra Hack by Konstantin Grcic. Besides bearing a strong connection to the theme, 'Hack' also served as the foundation for the event posters and invitations.

AREA X VITRA: WHAT THE HACK IS FUTURE?

What the hack
is future?

Warum die Arbeits-
welt von morgen eine
andere ist.

Etage Lumiere, Tabakfabrik Linz

6.10.2016
18.30 – 21.00

Raphael Gielgen
— Vitra
Head Research/
Trend Scouting

Timetable: 18.30–19.00 Doors Open 19.00–19.15 Eröffnungsworte
19.15–20.15 Raphael Gielgen 20.15–21.00 What the hack are they talking about

Akteure:
Raphael Gielgen, Wojciech Czaja (Moderation), Philip Rachinger (Mühltalhof)

RSVP Anmeldung unter: linz@area.at   AREA°   vitra.

Kooperationspartner

CREATIVE   afo   ORTNERSCHINKO   karriere.at   JⴲU
REGION   – A CREATIVE STUDIO

WORK TYPE | Branding, Collateral, Packaging
DESIGN | Jordan Richards

In Berlin, where locals really enjoy the art of the brew, Käfer: Coffee + Roaster stands out as a stylish one-stop coffee shop for roasted beans and handcrafted drinks. To complement the logomark designed after its namesake which means 'beetle' in German, Jordan Richards sought to man-ifest the exquisite craftsmanship exemplified by the team through a combination of glass, cardboard, and wooden materials. The results depicted a modern yet characterful brand that the city's discerning audience could appreciate.

KÄFER: COFFEE+ROASTER

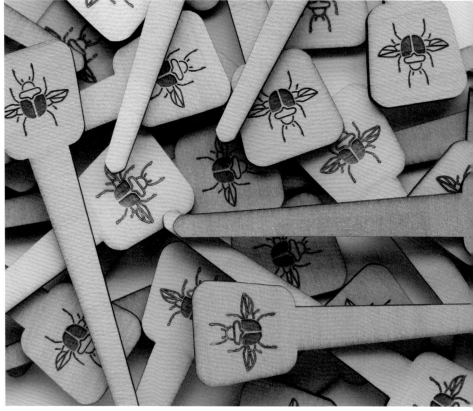

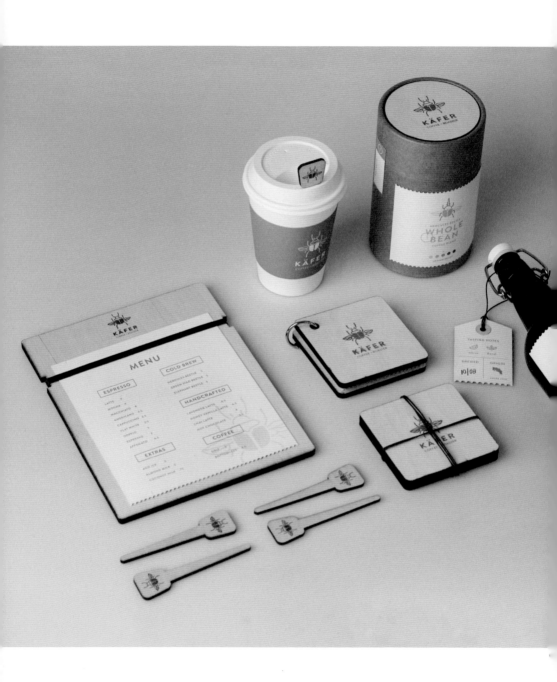

ALBUM
VERLAG
EDITION
CHRISTIAN
EISENBERGER

DREI BEMALTE
PAPIERBÖGEN GEFALTET
UND ZU 12 SEITEN
GEHEFTET, NUMMERIERT
UND SIGNIERT

WIEN IM
HERBST 2017   12/ 40+4

HIER
ÖFFNEN

WORK TYPE | Book, Packaging
DESIGN | Studio Riebenbauer
CLIENT | Christian Eisenbergwerk,
Album Verlag
PHOTOGRAPHY | Patrick Tafner

Inhabiting the space be-
tween art and book design,
Christian Eisenberger's
'Drei bemalte Papierbögen
Gefaltet und zu 12 Seiten
Geheftet, Nummeriert und
Signiert', which translates
to 'Three Painted Paper
Sheets Folded and Stapled
into 12 Pages, Numbered
and Signed', was created

to push the boundaries
in publishing. As the title
suggests, three original
paintings were folded into
12 pages and enclosed in
a wooden box, culminating
in a unique collaborative
outcome between Studio
Riebenbauer and art-book
publisher Album Verlag.

CHRISTIAN
EISENBERGER'S 'DREI
BEMALTE PAPIERBÖGEN'

EFTLING

BE, LEIM, MAKULATUR,
UNG, SCHICHTUNG, TAT
KLEBUNG, ORDNUNG
ND, IRRATIONALITÄT
NG, TRANSFORMATION
INDIVIDUALISIERUNG
G, AUSREIZUNG, TAT
KONFUSION, SÜNDTHESE
ERUNG, NOTWENDIGKEIT
H, GEBUNDEN, LIEBE
BERFLÄCHE, MÜLL
PAPIER, ROSTSCHUTZFARBE
RTLOS, LAPRIG, FETZN
VORBILDLOS, HALT-
NGSLOS, VEREINNAHMT,
LUNG, ENDLOS, SIEG,
GSLOS, VERWEIGERUNG,
SIGKEIT, HARMLOS,
OBERFLÄCHE, BIER
EINFLUSS, VISKOSITÄT,
CKSICHTSLOS, STOLPERN
NTENTIONSLOS, SUMPF
R, WERTBEFREIT
E, FAMILIE, LEUCHTTURM
NGSLOS, GEDÄCHTNIS,
N, EXIL, FREIHEIT?
LEUCHTTURM, LIEBE
HAFT, KONTROLLE
FNIS, DISNEY,
H, AUTHENTIZITÄT
SEN, FIGURAL

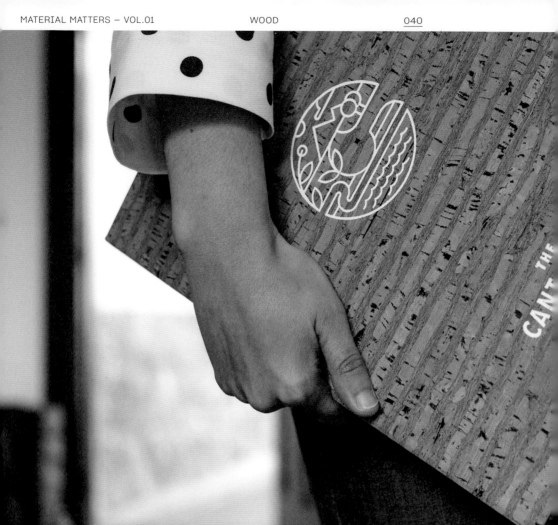

WORK TYPE | Branding, Stationery
DESIGN | Mubien Studio
CLIENT | The Cantabrian

Comprising the first sustainably managed eco-apartments of their kind in the region, The Cantabrian provides visitors in northern Spain with an authentic experience. In reflecting the company's love for nature as well as local customs, Mubien Studio created a modern visual identity that featured recognisable elements from the environment. They also used natural cork and recycled paper as the base materials in handcrafting the brand stationery to manifest its philosophies.

THE CANTABRIAN

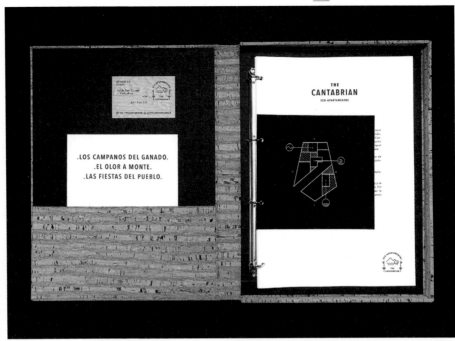

HERBERT ELSENWENGER
T / 06? S 84 66
M 0664 63 60 009
DORF 13 / 5301 EUGENDORF
TISCHLEREI@ELSENWENGER.AT
WWW.ELSENWENGER.AT

WORK TYPE | Branding, Collateral
DESIGN | Studio Riebenbauer
CLIENT | Tischlerei Elsenwenger
PHOTOGRAPHY | Patrick Tafner

Tischlerei Elsenwenger's visual identity characterises the precise and personalised nature of his craft as a carpenter. By featuring wood as an obvious reference to his profession and his favourite place in the world i.e. his workshop, Studio Riebenbauer succinctly captures his love for the material in a visceral way. They also applied his signature across all the branded collateral by emulating the dimension markings that he typically makes with chalk on his woodwork to reflect his attention to detail.

TISCHLEREI ELSENWENGER

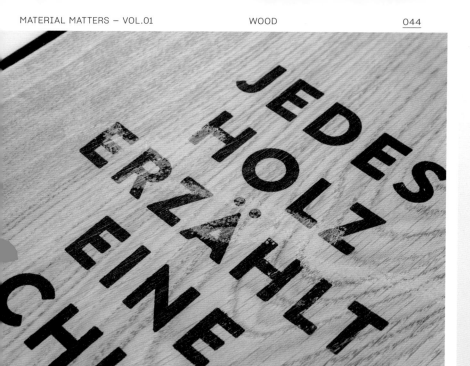

WORK TYPE | Trophy
DESIGN | Zoo Studio
CLIENT | Pujolasos

For the 2017 Luxe Pack New York trade fair, Pujolasos - a wooden cap manufacturer in the perfumery, cosmetics, and beverages industries - was invited to design and produce two trophies for the most 'green' participants. Inspired by the award category and the fair location, Zoo Studio constructed the New York city skyline out of 100% sustainable materials to form the body of the trophies. The unvarnished wooden pieces used were worked naturally, handcrafted, and all duly marked to show their origins.

LUXE PACK
NEW YORK AWARDS

WORK TYPE | Packaging
DESIGN | Backbone Branding

Pchak is a line of natural snacks that includes specialty nuts and dried fruit. In conceptualising its packaging design, Backbone Branding set out to root their idea in reality and steer clear of unnecessary visual elements. Deriving inspiration from the brand name itself, which refers to a tree hollow in Armenian, they found a clever way to inject a pure slice of nature into urban daily life while reflecting the freshness of the ingredients found within each box.

PCHAK

WORK TYPE | Product, Packaging
DESIGN | Power-nap Over Design Studio

Powerfully Natural Scent No.1 is a lemongrass-scented wax candle that can be used to spruce up any living space. In making the candle more than just about its fragrance, Power-nap Over Design Studio developed a simple yet striking packaging concept by wrapping each candle with printed transparent paper and screen-printing the brand's visual identity onto wooden cases. The interaction and resulting juxtaposition of both layers added depth and dimension to the overall design.

N.Y.N X P.N.O POWERFULLY NATURAL SCENT NO.1

WORK TYPE | Branding, Stationery
DESIGN | HMMM CREATIVE STUDIO
CLIENT | Groveneer
MATERIAL DESIGN | Mihkel Masso

Groveneer was created to transform the way a surface could look and feel without the need for any tool. Made from natural oak, it works as a sticker that can be used to cover or decorate walls, furniture, and the like by way of an easy peel-and-paste solution. To highlight its clever concept, HMMM CREATIVE STUDIO designed the brand's business cards by UV-printing information onto the material itself, so that potential customers could obtain a colour sample and try out its adhesive function at the same time.

GROVENEER

WORK TYPE | Packaging
DESIGN | For brands.
CLIENT | Message Candles

The contemporary-luxe look and feel of Message Candles's product range is a manifestation of its candle glasses' subtle elegance. Intrigued by the candles' wooden wick, For brands. were inspired to use the same wood to develop the brand's visual identity and packaging de-sign. Besides experimenting with wooden veneers of various sizes to achieve the best finish, they also creat-ed a set of unique picto-grams for the instruction booklet in each box to add character and charm.

MESSAGE CANDLES

message candles
message candles

message candles
message candles
message candles

WORK TYPE | Branding, Collateral
DESIGN | Bureau Rabensteiner
CLIENT | Nadine Von der Thannen

Hotel Trofana Alpin was the first what eventually became a group of family-owned properties in Ischgl, a popular winter sports resort in Austria. Local studio Bureau Rabensteiner were tasked to update the brand's look and feel while preserving the founders' heritage and spirit of hospitality as well as the essence of the location. They created an apt visual identity that revolved around its exemplary ability to balance tradition with modern conveniences and understated luxury amidst its alpine surroundings.

HOTEL TROFANA ALPIN

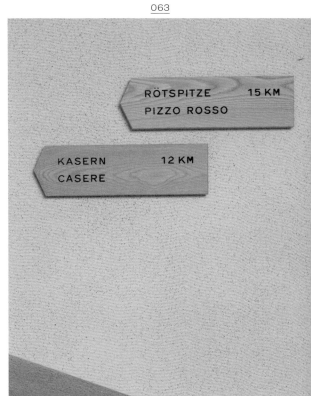

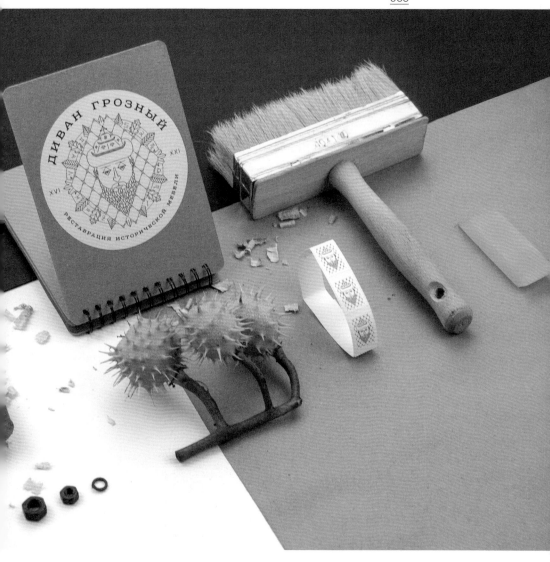

ДИВАН ГРОЗНЫЙ

XVI XXI

РЕСТАВРАЦИЯ ИСТОРИЧЕСКОЙ МЕБЕЛИ

WORK TYPE | Branding, Collateral
DESIGN | Dmytro Khrunevych

For Divan Grozny, a company specialising in refurbishing centuries-old furniture, Dmytro Khrunevych sought to embody the concept of longevity within its visual identity by combining several meaningful design ideas on wood. In addition to an illustration of the legendary Ivan Grozny or Ivan the Terrible who shares the same last name, its logo also featured zodiac signs, elements that were said to embellish Ivan's throne, to symbolise the reversal of time in referencing the company's craft of returning furniture to their prior pristine state.

DIVAN GROZNY

WORK TYPE | Type
DESIGN | Craig Ward

Inspired by the pagans' traditional way of life where stories or learnings were passed down through word of mouth instead of in writing, Craig Ward created a unique typeface that incorporated elements of tree worship, which was common in their culture. The PAGAN series featured the juxtaposition of clean, classically designed typography with the chaos of natural processes and materials that, when combined, created a visual tension. To apply the type onto wood by hand, he used pyrography, an old arts and crafts technique dating back to the fourth century.

PAGAN

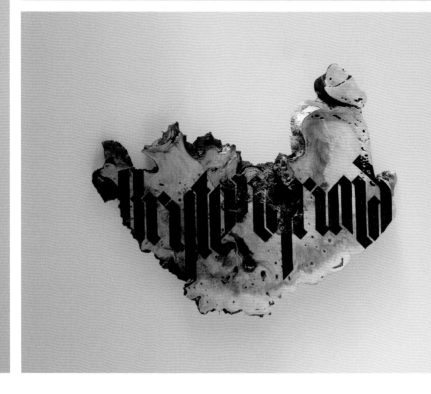

WORK TYPE | Packaging
DESIGN | 1 Trick Pony
CLIENT | Taft's Ale House
PRINTING | Steinhauser

In celebration of its first anniversary, Taft's Ale House in Ohio released a limited-edition Russian Imperial Stout that was aged for a year in bourbon barrels called Old Wooden Tooth. 1 Trick Pony teamed up with Steinhauser, a family-owned printing company that specialises in the beer and spirits industry, to create a customised wooden box for every 500mL bottle. Each box featured a branded neck flag and custom-printed labels that came in various striking colour combinations.

OLD WOODEN TOOTH

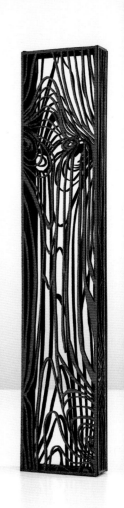

WORK TYPE | Art
ARTWORK | Studio Simone Post
PHOTOGRAPHY | Ronald Smits
COLLECTIVE | Envisions

Simone Post's interest in the image and identity of wood began upon encountering a world of contrasts at the Finsa factories, where stacks of tree trunks were shreded to become MDF while advanced machines were producing digital prints that mimicked wood convincingly. Through

Wannabe Wood, she sought to redirect the tension between the natural and artificial by intentionally recreating woodgrains with colourful graphic prints. She also used a CNC machine to mill individual rings and form a bas-relief; unveiling the underlying fibre layers for realistic finishes.

WANNABE WOOD

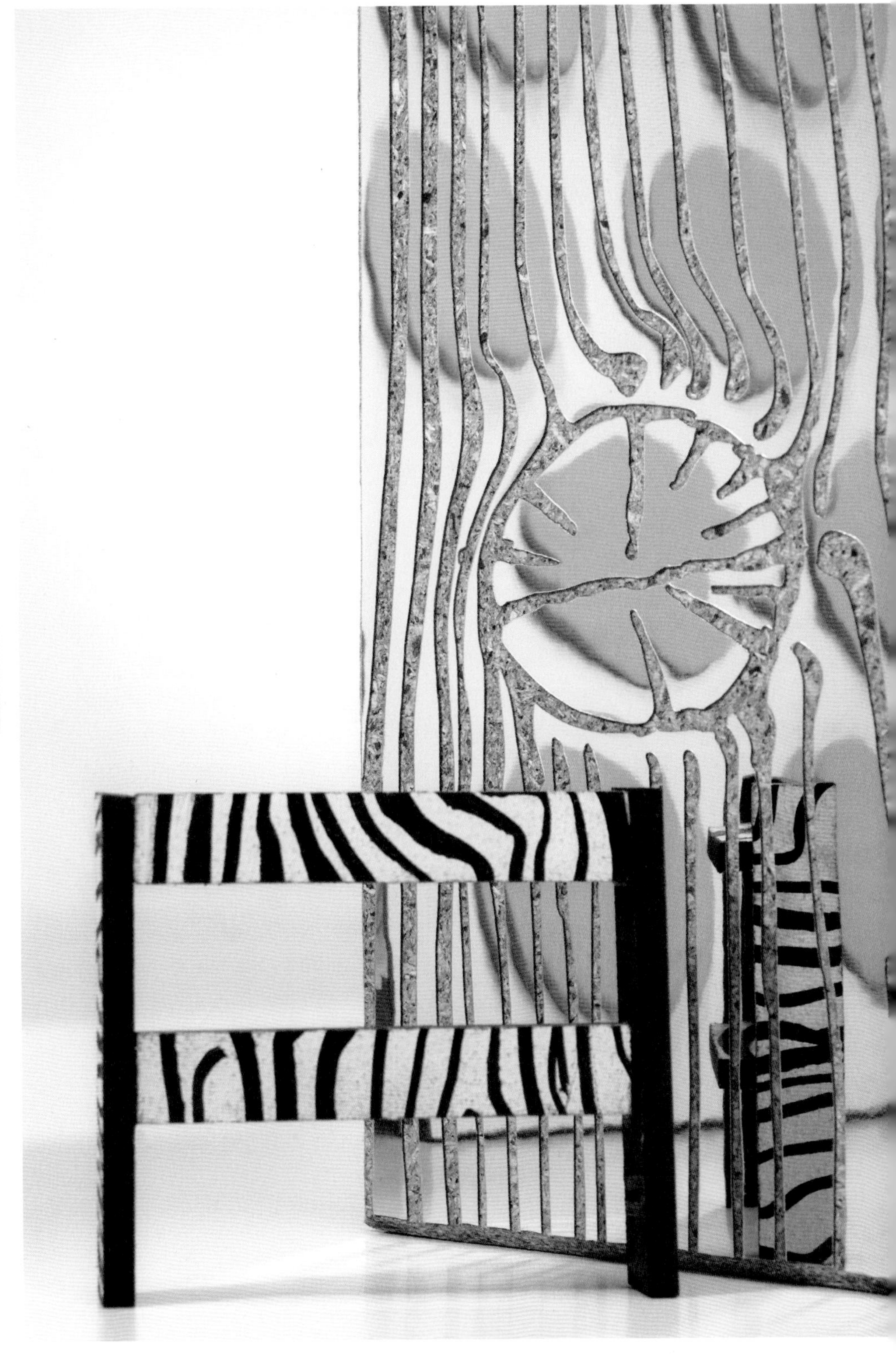

WORK TYPE | Product
DESIGN | Lex Pott, New Window

Objects under the Diptych collection were all derived from the principle of 'unravelling a tree's hidden history by laying its annual rings bare'. Commissioned by New Window, Rotterdam-based designer Lex Pott utilised a single Douglas fir that was planted and felled in Veluwe for this truly 'made in the Netherlands' collaboration. Featuring unique patterns from sandblasting, natural variances, and intricate markings, it manifested the juxtaposition between organic and geometric shapes, open and closed parts, as well as control and freedom.

DIPTYCH

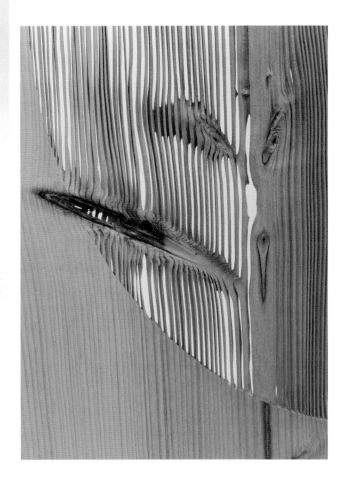

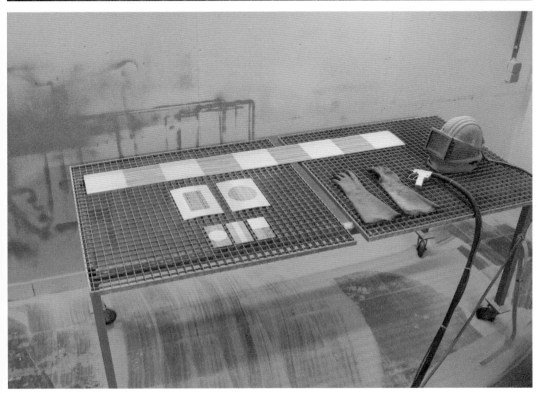

WORK TYPE | Branding, Collateral
DESIGN | Heydays
CLIENT | Skovin Gulv

Skovin Gulv provides a variety of high-end wood flooring solutions for the premium residential market. Besides giving it a name that was inspired by its company location, Heydays sought to reflect the quality and craftsmanship that the brand stands for by creating a visual identity based on the idea that floor surfaces can define a room. They used wooden pieces to represent the main component of the business, and combined the material's warm tones with red visual elements as a contemporary touch.

SKOVIN GULV

WORK TYPE | Branding, Collateral
CLIENT | Linden Baum Co., Ltd.
ART DIRECTION | NOSIGNER
GRAPHIC DESIGN | NOSIGNER
SWEETS DESIGN | Linden Baum Co., Ltd.
SPACE DESIGN | NOSIGNER,
Aki Hamada Architects Inc
PHOTOGRAPHY | Ohako Studio

Led by Eisuke Tachikawa, the NOSIGNER team was tasked to revitalise the Uozu Buried Forest Museum, a secluded venue located 2.5 hours away from Tokyo. In designing a new visual identity that would create a buzz and impact the surrounding areas, they drew upon the Buried Forest itself, where trees eventually become fossils in the sand. To refresh the museum's brand image while showcasing the unusual natural treasure it was built for, their work featured a contemporary graphic system amidst a vibrant green palette.

KININAL

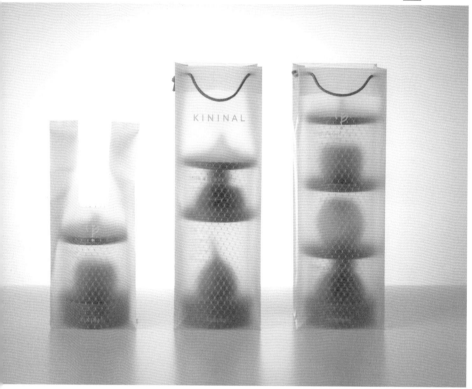

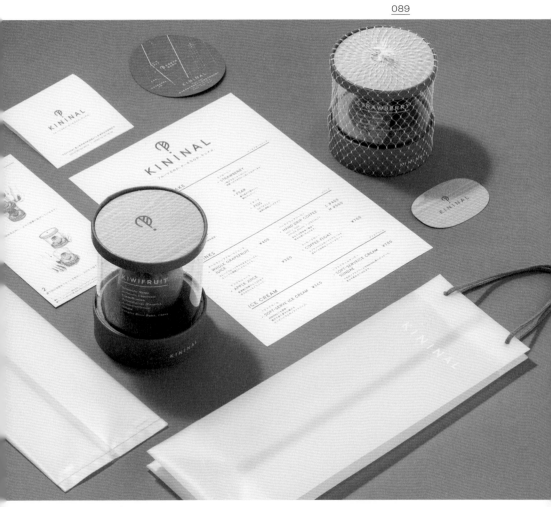

WORK TYPE | Trophy, Collateral
DESIGN | Garbett
CLIENT | CareerTrackers
PRINTING | Green & Gold
LASER-ETCHING | The Laser Co.
PRODUCTION | Flitch and Rasp

CareerTrackers is an Australian non-profit organisation that addresses indigenous disadvantage by developing professional career pathways, internship programmes, and links with private sector employers. It honours the successes of students and philanthropy partners at an annual gala awards event with over 2,000 attendees. For its eighth edition, Garbett created a cohesive visual identity revolving around the concept of building blocks; featuring simple shapes in vibrant colours to reflect a future of infinite possibilities.

CAREERTRACKERS
AWARDS IDENTITY

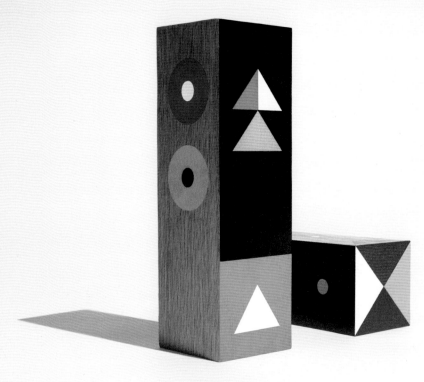

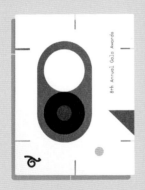

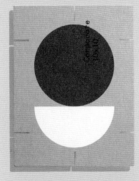

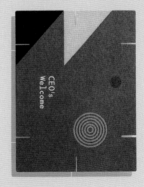

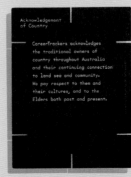

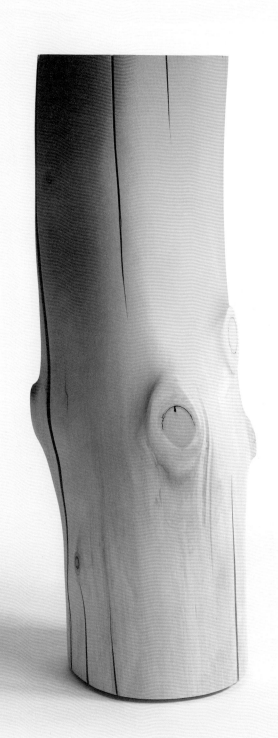

WORK TYPE | Art
ARTWORK | Katia Jacquet

Born into a family where her grandfather was a sculptor and wood was always a part of daily life, artist Katia Jacquet set out to celebrate the material's soft, rough, and delicate qualities. With Lovebuch, she presented a series of unique artpieces that were each signed, dated, and authenticated with the GPS locations of their log extraction sites. Although they were enhanced with modern graphic motifs and techniques, she was careful to remain respectful of the original wood; giving her creations a deeper sense of meaning.

LOVEBUCH

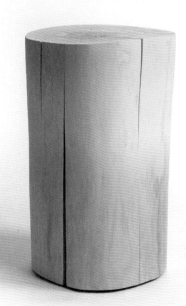

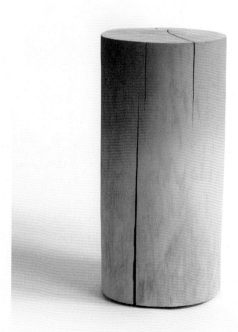

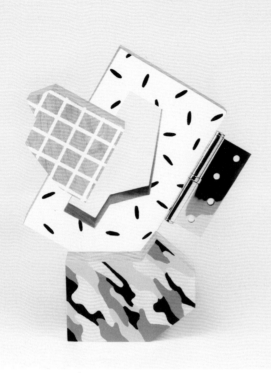

WORK TYPE | Branding, Collateral
DESIGN | A-2-0 design studio
CLIENT | Bereza

Bereza or 'birch tree' in Russian is a milling workshop that produces bespoke furniture and household items. For its visual identity, A-2-0 design studio cut various shapes out of a single wooden block to reflect a milling machine's main function as well as to create various sculptures and patterns that could be used to form its logo and supporting elements. They also arranged the letters in its logotype to resemble an abstract imprint of a birch tree bark and emphasise the brand's distinct sense of individuality.

BEREZA

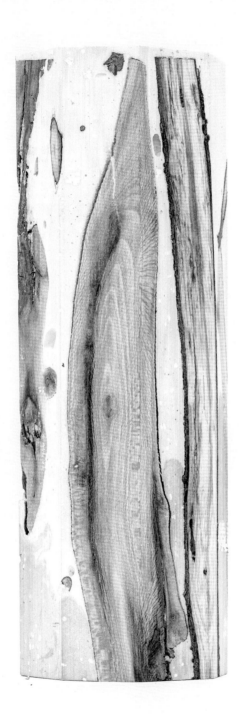

WORK TYPE | Product
DESIGN | Benwu Studio

The Living Material project explores new design methods in repurposing the most basic natural materials to discover their potential and visualise the beauty of nature in innovative ways. For their Twig Vessel collection, Benwu Studio mixed different twigs and branches to not only achieve many unpredictable outcomes, but also depict the contrasts between each material on an industrial scale. Through the experiment, they found new applications for wood without losing functionality or durability to aesthetics.

TWIG VESSEL

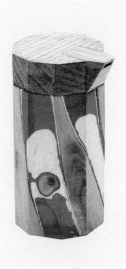

GREEK STYLE
STATOS
MANOURI GOAT CHEESE

STATOS
MANOURI GOAT CHEESE

WORK TYPE | Packaging
DESIGN | Jialu Li

For Staios Goat Cheese's packaging design, Jialu Li was inspired by the brand name's origins. Besides being a derivation of the Greek word which means 'most excellent' or 'most useful', Aristaios is also said to be the name of the rustic god of shepherds, cheese-making, beekeeping, and honey. Coupling this whimsical narrative with its mission to deliver the finest cheese in the US, her intricate illustrations and etchings reflected the brand's diligence, passion, and attention to detail.

STAIOS CHEESE
PACKAGING DESIGN

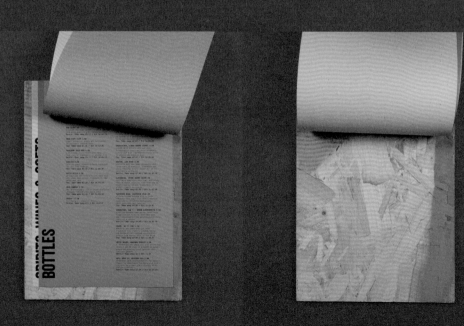

WORK TYPE | Menu
DESIGN | O Street
CLIENT | BrewDog
ARTWORK | BrewDog Team
PRINTING | Windmill Printing

Best known for its beers and attitude, BrewDog needed a consistent yet compelling menu system for over 50 bars across the UK and the US. In reflecting the brand's true guerilla-punk spirit, O Street gathered a group of Brew-Dog employees and set them loose with spray paint on wooden boards. On top of the unique pieces of art that they ended up with afterwards, letterpress-printed elements were added onto the menu papers to create a cohesive authentically crafted look.

BREWDOG BAR MENUS

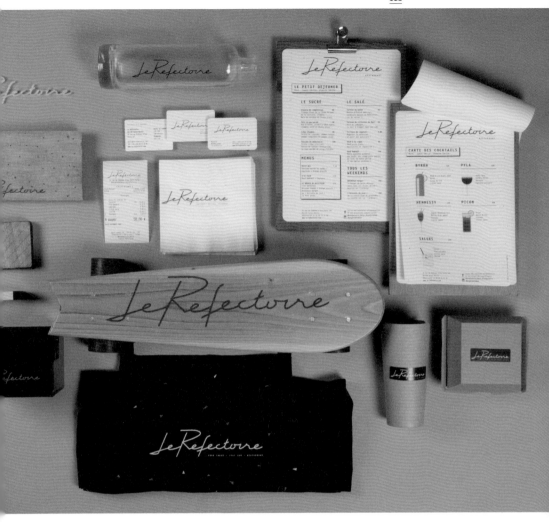

WORK TYPE | Branding, Collateral
DESIGN | Yorgo&Co
CLIENT | Le Refectoire
PHOTOGRAPHY | Louis David Najar

The team behind popular Parisian food truck company Le Refectoire were looking to expand through catering and permanent restaurants. Yorgo&Co were tasked to create a new visual identity that would reflect the brand's growth without overshadowing its existing work.

Starting with a script logotype that could translate well into neon signs and typography-driven designs, they developed a stylish branding system that was further enhanced with a colourful confetti pattern and wooden materials.

LE REFECTOIRE

WORK TYPE | Exhibition
DESIGN | dn&co
CLIENT | St James's Pavilion
PHOTOGRAPHY | Tian Khee Siong
ILLUSTRATION | James Graham
ANIMATRONICS | John Nolan Studio
PRODUCTION | 2MZ

To celebrate St James's Market's regeneration and rich history, dn&co sought to retell a forgotten 300-year-old tale about The Handsome Butcher through an exhibition inspired by Victorian paper theatre. Combining illustrations, sound design, animatronics by the studio responsible for the Harry Potter films as well as narrations by Stephen Fry, they crafted a memorable multi-sensorial experience featuring over 300 laser-cut wooden scenes that filled more than 100 cabinets in total.

THE HANDSOME BUTCHER

WORK TYPE | Packaging
DESIGN | Grantipo
CLIENT | OAK wine

In winemaking, fermentation plays a key role in determining the quality of the outcome. Knowing this, Grantipo were intrigued by the idea of creating bottles made from the same wood that was used for the cask, so as to not disrupt the ingredients' cycle of fermentation. Through their OAK wine initiative, they succeeded in storing the wine consistently from the beginning to the end of the process in a thoughtful and sophisticated manner.

OAK WINE

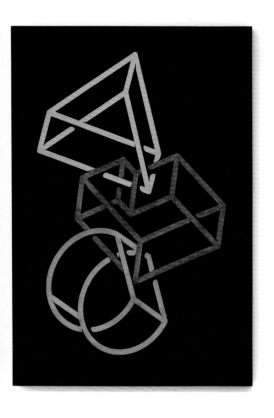

WORK TYPE | Art
ARTWORK | eltipo
PHOTOGRAPHY | Brigitte De Puydt,
Tom Verstraeten

In April 2017, eltipo held his second solo art exhibition entitled 'Don't Believe The Type' in Antwerp. Inspired by his experiences while working for commercial brands where products were typically 'hyped up' or promoted, he depicted the mishmash of information that modern consumers typically have to absorb or process in a visceral way. His unique messages were brought to life through a mixture of materials that were laser-engraved, cut, and assembled by hand.

DON'T BELIEVE THE TYPE

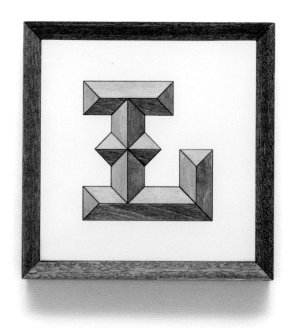

WORK TYPE | Artwork
DESIGN | eltipo
SPECIAL CREDIT | J Dilla

J Dilla, or James Dewitt Yancey, was an American record producer and rapper who emerged in the mid-1990s and left a strong legacy in hip hop culture before he died. As part of a group exhibition held to pay tribute to the artist and celebrate his talent, eltipo created wooden inlay artworks featuring shapes, patterns, and typography in a variety of wooden shapes and shades. The effects of different materials, layers, and letters coming together epitomised J Dilla's legendary sampling techniques.

J DILLA TRIBUTE

WORK TYPE | Art
ARTWORK | Graci Studio
PHOTOGRAPHY | Josh Leclaire

Graci Studio found a creative way to produce beautiful works of art out of the various hardwood off-cuts that could be found at their local sawmills and cabinet shops. After carving squares from the wood, they then burned or painted the surfaces to enhance existing textures or make new ones. All of the square pieces were cut using the same measurements and could be combined in any direction to create personalised masterpieces.

CARVED SQUARES

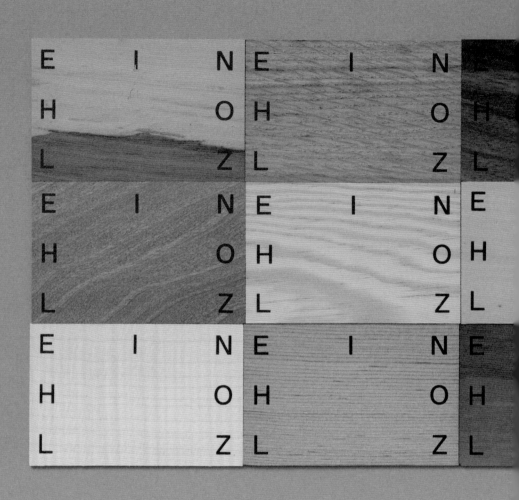

WORK TYPE | Branding, Stationery, Web
DESIGN | Bureau Collective
CLIENT | Einholz
FONT | Favorit von Dinamo

Ueli Reusser is a woodwork expert and an independent carpenter who specialises in joinery. For his brand Einholz or 'unicorn' in English, Bureau Collective set out to highlight his core expertise with a visual identity featuring a flexible grid that reflected the all-encompassing nature of his daily tasks through the agility with which the grid could be applied onto any rectangular shape. They also created business cards using real woodcuts from his archive; making each one a truly unique piece.

EINHOLZ

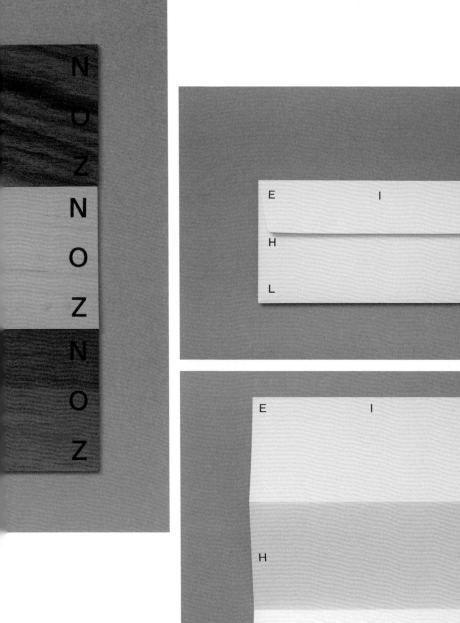

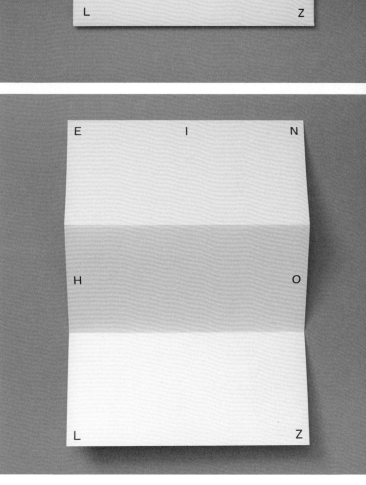

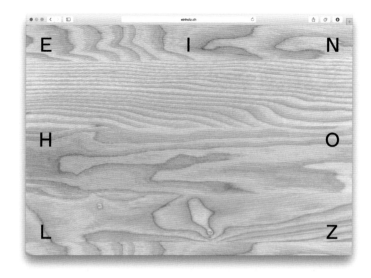

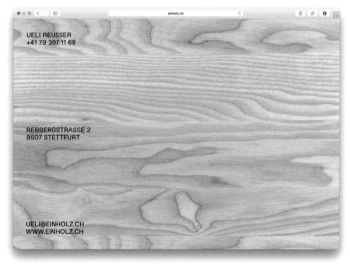

UELI REUSSER
+41 79 397 11 68

REBBERGSTRASSE 2
9507 STETTFURT

UELI@EINHOLZ.CH
WWW.EINHOLZ.CH

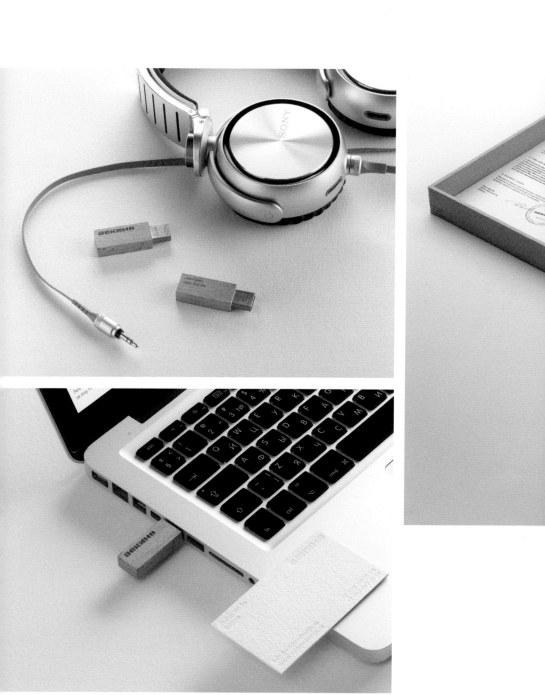

WORK TYPE | Branding, Collateral
DESIGN | Comence design studio
CLIENT | Eskimo
PHOTOGRAPHY | Andrey Pleshkov

In the Russian language, the word 'eskimo' actually refers to iced chocolate. Inspired by this concept, Comence design studio created an apt visual identity for Eskimo by juxtaposing a minimalist-chic style with a maximum focus on production technologies. They selected high-quality materials like African mahogany veneer sheets as well as Fedrigoni Nettuno Carruba and Nero papers in a range of 'iced-chocolate' hues to reflect the meaning behind the brand's name.

ESKIMO IDENTITY

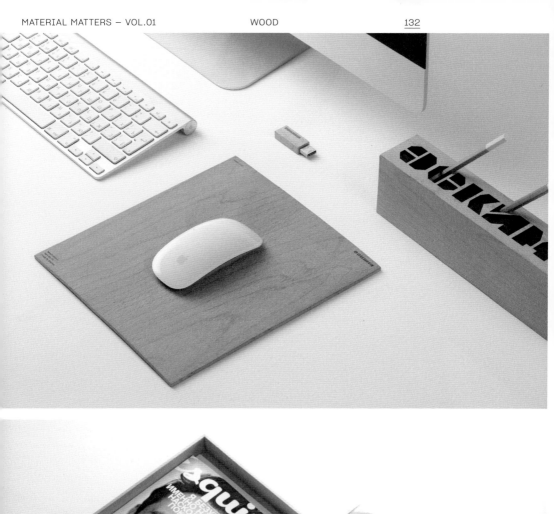

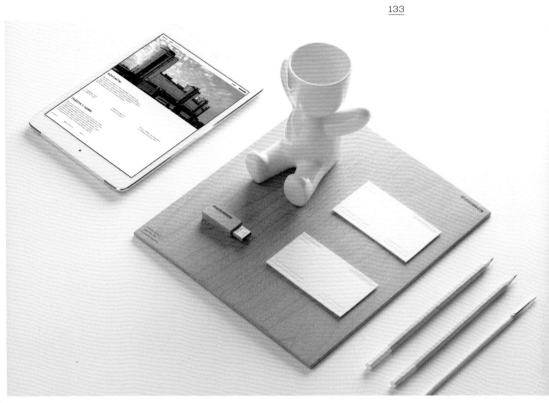

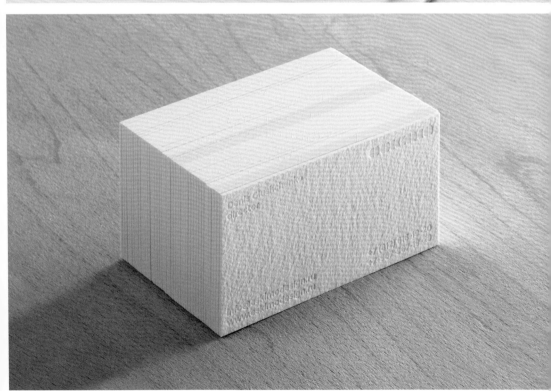

WORK TYPE | Packaging
DESIGN | Grand Deluxe
CLIENT | Clef

Inspired by the forest industry in the Ehime prefecture, Grand Deluxe's timber-like design work for Petit Clef's Baumkuchen packaging revolved around the annual rings of trees. The name of the town where the café is located - Kuma - is also the homonym for the word 'bear' in Japanese, which was why the animal was characterised on the box as a pâtissier. When displayed side-by-side, the boxes visually resembled stacked lumber; promoting local produce in a meaningful and memorable way.

KUMAYAMA, BEAR & BAUMKUCHEN

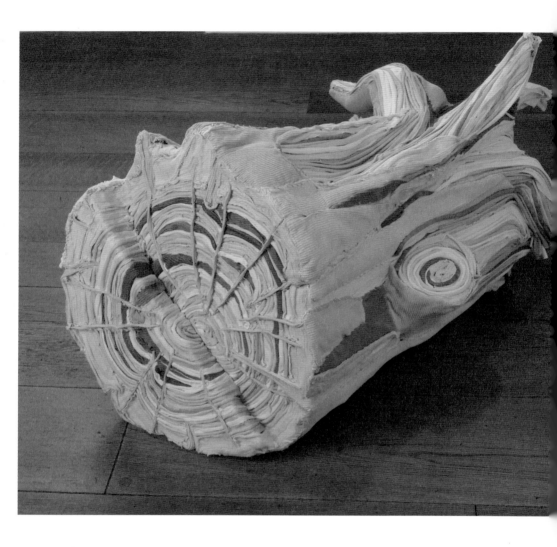

WORK TYPE | Art
ARTWORK | Tamara Kostianovsky
PHOTOGRAPHY | Roni Mocan

Tamara Kostianovsky's tree sculptures blended form and meaning in a fascinating way. By creating severed tree stumps of different shapes and sizes in a range of colours indicative of human insides, her work re-imagined the Earth's landscape as a severed body to depict the concept of regeneration. In all her pieces, she used articles of clothing that belonged to her late father to embody the passing of time, feelings of loss, and the final integration of flesh to dust and the landscape.

TREE STUMPS

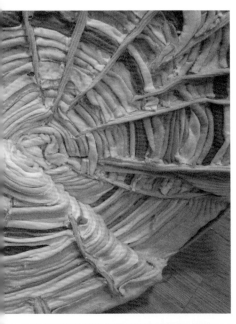

WORK TYPE | Product
DESIGN | Elisa Strozyk
PHOTOGRAPHY | STUDIO BEEN

Through her experimental designs, Elisa Strozyk seeks to push the boundaries of materials in both form and function. Using wood, a hard material that typically cannot be manipulated by touch as a foundation, she created a new half-wood, half-textile material that 'smells familiar, feels strange, and moves in unexpected ways'. By playing with the geometry and size of the tiles made from deconstructed wooden pieces, her wooden textiles reflect flexibility, mobility, and a myriad of sculptural possibilities.

WOODEN TEXTILES

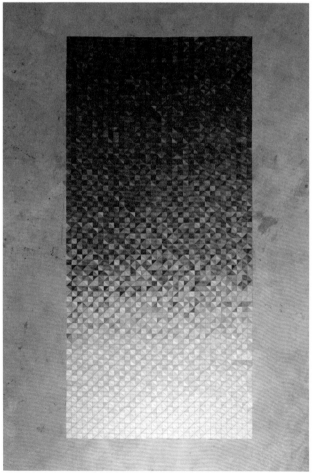

WORK TYPE | Branding, Stationery
DESIGN | Mubien Studio
CLIENT | Niditas

Niditas is an equestrian hotel specialising in romantic surprises. For its visual identity development, Mubien worked with owners Noelia and Octavia who were both likened to chickadees, which are birds that can starve themselves before they would ever leave their partner. Inspired by the animals' behaviour, the concept for Niditas revolved around helping couples experience love at its best. In reflecting the brand's authenticity, Mubien handcrafted all of its stationery using textured papers, wood, and leather with bronze stamping.

NIDITAS

WORK TYPE | Packaging
DESIGN | mistroom
CLIENT | TREE OF LIFE

Tree of Life is a Taiwanese band whose album, 'We Are Imperfect', was released in 2014. Tasked with designing a cover that reflected the album's concept of exploring and embracing one's inner truth, mistroom likened people to 'weeds that could find their way through cracks in the wall' as a testament to their strength and fortitude in life. In translating the idea onto the album booklet, they left the edges of its pages untrimmed; resulting in an authentic design that embodied the unique beauty of imperfection.

WE ARE IMPERFECT

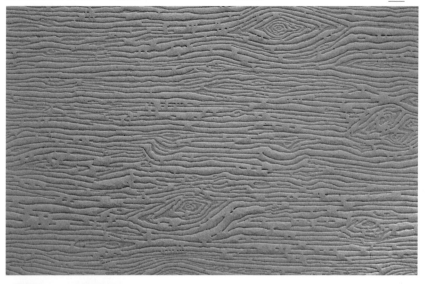

WORK TYPE | Book
DESIGN | Passport
CLIENT | NatWest

'How to Grow A Branch' by NatWest depicted the meaningful design concept behind one of the company's latest sustainability-focused branches. It contained stories of the fabrics, materials, and furniture used in the building process, and served to answer any question that a customer could have about the space. In bringing the book to life, Passport drew inspiration from nature and sought to illustrate elements from the environment in a visceral and visually compelling way.

NATWEST:
HOW TO GROW A BRANCH

WORK TYPE | Product, Packaging
DESIGN | ACRE Design Pte Ltd
CLIENT | Banyan Tree
ADDITIONAL DESIGN | Banyan Tree Gallery
Design Team

As part of Banyan Tree Group's mission to inspire a lifestyle interwoven with wellness, the Banyan Tree Essentials beauty and body care line is formulated with the best of nature. ACRE Design Pte Ltd's rebranding work featured new signature bottles with a distinct asymmetrical silhouette as well as an homage to the first banyan found in the group's first flagship hotel. To reflect the brand's ethos on sustainability, they also designed fabric wraps woven with used plastic bottles and boxes handmade with mulberry papers as gift packaging.

BANYAN TREE ESSENTIALS

WORK TYPE | Packaging
DESIGN | Daniel Lindqvist

Basis believes in developing environmentally responsible formulas without making any compromises. In designing a visual identity that would reflect how honest, natural, and high-quality its soaps and polishes are, Daniel Lindqvist used a sustainable yet striking cardboard material that allowed for its products to stand out on the shelves. He also chose various shades of wood to represent the different ranges and add a sense of warmth to appeal to potential customers.

BASIS

WORK TYPE | Art
ARTWORK | AFTSTUDIO

Marquetry involves cutting wood veneer by hand and fitting the pieces together to create unique surface pattern designs; an intricate process that combines woodwork, collaging, and painting. AFTSTUDIO's Camouflage series presented a number of abstract patterns that were both graphic and organic in nature. The project took the textural elements of old marquetry landscapes that typically depict idyllic pastoral scenes to the next level by enlarging and abstracting them into more vibrant and contrasting decorative pieces.

VENEER MARQUETRY

THE
MATERIAL
—

WOOD *(n.)*

UK & US /wʊd/
[countable or uncountable]

a hard substance that forms the branches and trunks of trees and
can be used as a building material, for making things, or as a fuel

TYPES

STRUCTURE

KEY PROPERTIES

SUSTAINABILITY

TYPES

When it comes to natural wood, there is a strong correlation between its inherent characteristics and the characteristics of the tree that yielded it. For instance, how dense or thick it is depends on its species, which would in turn determine its mechanical capabilities or how it is best used.

According to a comprehensive study of the world's plants, there were more than 60,000 tree species in the world as of 2017. Although there has been a surge in the production of manufactured boards or processed timber such as medium density fibreboards (MDF), plywood, and chipboards in recent times, natural wood can generally be classified under:

HARDWOODS

These woods typically come from broad-leaved or deciduous trees that seasonally shed leaves (usually in the autumn) and have their seeds encased in fruits or pods. They have distinct gains that make them suitable for making furniture and decorative woodwork with. Examples: Ash, beech, birch, mahogany, maple, oak, teak, walnut.

SOFTWOODS

These woods typically come from evergreen or coniferous trees that have needles and cones that they retain year-round. They are better suited for construction work in the form of planks and poles. Although their names suggest otherwise, some hardwoods are actually softer than softwoods. Examples: Cedar, cypress, fir, pine, spruce, redwood.

STRUCTURE

As an organic material, wood is chemically composed of cells like any other plant. These cells comprise three substances known as 'cellulose' which is broadly referred to as the fibrous bulk of a tree, 'lignin' which is the adhesive that holds the fibres together, and the remainder, 'hemicellulose'.

Beyond its cells, the tangible inner structure of a tree determines what its wood is like in form and function. Each of these components has a purpose that can be drawn upon to add depth and dimension to a creative project or construction.

BARK

The outer skin of wood from a tree that can be 'peeled' to reveal two kinds of wood within (i.e. sapwood and heartwood).

SAPWOOD

The light and moist layer closest to the inner bark that is full of xylem (i.e. tubes that help a tree transport water and nutrients from its roots to its leaves).

HEARTWOOD

The dark and dry innermost layer beyond the sapwood that has no xylem.

ANNUAL / GROWTH RINGS

The lines that denote how old a tree is, as seen when its trunk is sliced horizontally. As the sapwood grows outwards, a new ring is added each year.

GRAINS

The lines that run parallel to the xylem, as seen when its trunk is sliced vertically.

KNOTS

The oval shapes that interrupt the grains and denote where branches grew out from the trunk.

KEY PROPERTIES

STRONG

Wood is a solid yet malleable material. It can be cut, bent, or snapped, but not compressed or stretched in opposite directions due to its anisotropic nature. To capitalise on its tensile strength, one needs to work with - rather than against - the grain by placing it upright or vertically as it offers more resistance this way; as opposed to placing it sideways or horizontally.

DURABLE

Although wood is an organic material that is subject to natural decay and rotting, where organisms like fungi, termites, and beetles gradually reduce it to dust, a wooden object can last for hundreds, or even thousands, of years; provided that it is properly preserved and protected from exposure to the elements.

POROUS & FIBROUS

Due to its structure, wood can swell up in damp conditions and dry out when the temperature rises; making it hygroscopic, or water absorbent in nature. It is also a poor conductor of heat and electricity, due to the lack of movable ions in its makeup. On the other hand, wood can used to absorb, transmit, and amplify sounds effectively - which is why it forms the basis of many musical instruments.

SUSTAINABILITY

As one of the most versatile materials available to mankind, wood continues to be an indispensable part of our daily lives. Although it is obtained and used for a variety of purposes, it has the potential to be completely sustainable in the future; but only if a new tree is planted for every tree cut down. Unfortunately, due to the fact that new trees possess less economic value than mature ones that have been growing for hundreds of years, irresponsible logging remains an issue all around the world.

Besides the obvious negative impact that clear-cutting a tropical rainforest or selective felling in temperate woodlands has on flora and fauna, certain forestry and woodworking practices have also been found to be detrimental to the environment at large; such as the pollution of rivers surrounding paper mills due to dumping of the chlorine used to bleach wood fibres. As much as manufactured wood substitutes are on the rise, the onus ultimately lies on us to adopt proper measures that conserve not only a precious natural resource, but also our planet as a whole.

All dictionary definitions are from dictionary.cambridge.org.
All information is correct as of 2019 from www.explainthatstuff.com, en.wikipedia.org, and studyread.com. Please visit the websites for more information and links to further resources.

1 Trick Pony
Pages 070-071

Much more than an advertising agency, a web design firm, or a graphic design company, 1 Trick Pony is a creative services shop that operates globally and on the WWW. Based in Philadelphia, they specialise in strategy, concepts, social media, interactive development, design, execution, and services management.

A-2-0 design studio
Pages 098-099

Established by four graphic designers with their own unique perspectives, A-2-0 design studio is driven by a strong desire to push, change, and break traditional boundaries using emotional substance. In creating work with compelling ideas that combine graphic design, photography, and fine art, it believes that a deep understanding of a project's core is of utmost importance; building new visual languages by adopting innovative and often-unusual materials and cutting-edge techniques.

ACRE Design Pte Ltd
Pages 152-153

Co-founded in 2011 by T Y Zheng and Jason Song, ACRE is a Singapore-based multidisciplinary strategy and brand consultancy. Besides creating identities, spaces, objects, and experiences, it also helps businesses with strategy, corporate identity guidelines, and brand architecture. Its approach balances three attributes of their rational decision-making process – pragmatism, empathy, and aesthetics.

AFTSTUDIO
Pages 011, 158-160

AFTSTUDIO is the contemporary woodwork practice of Josh Woolliscroft, who studied product design in Glasgow, Paris, and Stockholm. Currently based in East London, it uses traditional techniques of veneer marquetry and hand-carving to create decorative and functional homewares. Josh's work is born from a lifelong love of handcrafted wooden objects, a fondness for playful forms, as well as an obsession with sanding things smooth. Every piece is the result of an evolving interaction between hand and material.

Backbone Branding
Pages 050-051

Believing that brands are brought to life when their essence is expressed through design, Backbone Branding is an independent branding studio and creative business partner for clients who are ready for extraordinary solutions. They dig deep into the core of a brand to offer their clients undeniably relevant and incredibly engaging outcomes.

Benwu Studio
Pages 100-103

Founded in 2012 by designer Hongchao Wang and Peng You, Benwu Studio initially focused on material experiments and craft research. In 2015, joining forces with interior architect Ge Wei, product designer Qiyun Deng, and exhibition designer Penglong Geng, it became a multidisciplinary design agency with expertise and experience in product, set, and interior design. Currently based in both Shanghai and Beijing, the studio continues to work on a series of successful collaboration projects with renowned clients from around the world.

Bureau Collective

Pages 126-129

A multidisciplinary creative studio founded by Ollie Schaich and Ruedi Zürcher, Bureau Collective specialises in projects within the cultural field from their base in St. Gallen. Working with a wide range of global clients, they are driven by people as passionate as they are to deliver effective solutions that span the entire spectrum of graphic design.

Bureau Rabensteiner

Pages 060-063

Right in the heart of the Alps lies Bureau Rabensteiner, a branding and graphic design studio involved in everything from brand building to packaging and editorial work. Through strategic thinking and meaningful designs, the studio has built an international reputation for crafting high-quality solutions.

Comence design studio

Pages 130-133

Comence specialises in brand strategy, identity, web, mobile, and packaging design by working closely with its clients. The design studio strives to develop long-lasting relationships between brands and their customers through trust.

Craig Ward

Pages 066-069

Craig Ward is an award-winning design director currently based in New York. Besides being a studio owner, he is also an occasional artist, a best-selling author, public speaker, and contributor to various industry journals - best known for his pioneering typographic works. In 2015, Craig was named one of the most important designers of all time by Computer Arts magazine.

Daniel Lindqvist

Pages 154-157

After graduating in 2016 with a BFA in graphic design, Daniel Lindqvist has since worked as a designer at agencies like Manual, Side Cm, and Ammunition. He is passionate about his work and enjoys experimenting with typography, photography, as well as craftsmanship. When he is not working, he paints and listens to music.

Dmytro Khrunevych

Pages 013, 064-065

Obsessed with details, typography, and linework, Dmytro Khrunevych is a Kyiv-based graphic designer who loves colours and photography.

dn&co

Pages 114-115

Inspired by different cultures and places, dn&co creates meaningful spaces of all kinds. A brand and design consultancy dedicated to defeating the seemingly inexorable rise of easy monoculture, its every project is rooted in finding a deeper purpose and telling that story.

Elisa Strozyk

Pages 012, 140-143

German Design Award-winner Elisa Strozyk studied textile and surface design at the KHB in Berlin and completed an MA course in future textiles at Central Saint Martins in London before starting her own experimental practice. She constantly explores the boundaries between 2D and 3D as well as hard and soft materials, switching meanings and categories. Currently, Elisa is building bridges between textile- and furniture design, using wood to produce original textiles and objects.

Elisava Pack

ELISAVA is an institute of education and research affiliated with Pompeu Fabra University in Barcelona. Under its master's degree programme in packaging design known as Elisava Pack, students are tasked to develop a comprehensive packaging project encompassing the main processes of briefing, branding, and designing. Carine Attar and Anna Gené Casellas who combined their knowledge and experiences for the project featured.

eltipo

eltipo is an all-round independent artist who specialises in hand-drawn and vectorised lettering, illustration, and graphic design. His portfolio is an amalgamation of diverse skillsets translated across different platforms, featuring influences from various subcultures such as extreme sports, tattoo art, motocross, sign painting, and graffiti.

For brands.

Dedicated to making brands visible internationally, For brands. is an independent studio in Poland specialising in crafting brands online and offline. It creates comprehensive solutions that are simple yet intriguing in the details.

Garbett

Driven by a desire to make the world better and more delightful through design thinking, Garbett is a Sydney-based graphic design studio specialising in brand identity, art direction, and image-making. It works on various projects, whether they involve one-off image-making or complex identity programming.

Graci Studio

Exhibited and collected extensively throughout the US, Graci Studio's work aims to capture the beauty of nature and modern design by stripping down unnecessary elements and focusing on the simplicity and purity of the object.

Grand Deluxe

Founded in 2005 by Koji Matsumoto, Grand Deluxe is a graphic design studio based in Ehime. Specialising in the branding of products and local companies, it has won various international awards such as the ONE SHOW Gold, New York ADC Silver, and D&AD Bronze.

Grantipo

Grantipo is a Madrid-based design studio that specialises in branding and packaging. It strives to convert every project into something special by approaching each of them in a way that values the creative process as much as the final result. Offering solutions based on simple, functional, and coherent design, the team is constantly learning and experimenting with creativity without ever conforming to the norm.

Heydays

Heydays is a Norwegian creative studio that knows how to make wood look good. Its creative solutions revolve around showcasing the material in the most authentic and respectable way possible across various platforms.

HMMM CREATIVE STUDIO

A multidisciplinary design collective based in Tallinn, HMMM CREATIVE STUDIO specialises in branding and concept-based solutions.

Jialu Li

Pages 104–105

Specialising in visual development and branding, Jialu Li or Cece is a San Francisco-based designer who enjoys challenging herself and pushing boundaries. Besides designing impactful visuals, her creative process also allows her to learn more about herself and value the journey of designing itself.

Jordan Richards

Pages 032–035

Growing up, Jordan Richards was fascinated with the joy he experienced when holding well-designed products. His curiosity for the processes and people behind them led him to study design at Oklahoma State University. With a passion for interactive design, packaging design, and iconography, Jordan currently pursues visual design in the tech industry.

Katia Jacquet

Pages 094–097

Before founding Stereochromie in Paris, Katia Jacquet grew up in the Jura mountains and studied the decorative arts in Strasbourg. Constantly questioning the meaning of objects and the energy that they radiate, she is fascinated by the craftsman's gesture and always feels the need to connect with materials. Her passion for nature influences and nourishes her work.

Lex Pott

Pages 015, 078–083

Rotterdam-based experimental designer Lex Pott employs a raw and intuitive method in his work by returning to the origins of the materials he uses most: wood, stone, and metal. A graduate of the Design Academy Eindhoven, he does not hide his designs under indirect layers.

mistroom

Pages 148–149

Founded in 2010 by designers Yu-jui Peng and Jui-i Huang, mistroom in Taiwan specialises in design work for the performing arts sector, as well as book binding, vinyl design, and packaging design.

Mubien Studio

Pages 040–041, 144–147

Mubien is a design studio and workshop specialising in branding for international clients. Besides helping new businesses and brands, it also revitalises and revolutionises existing ones through carefully crafted design and strategy.

NOSIGNER

Pages 086–089

Yokohama-based design agency NOSIGNER defines itself as a social activist that pursues the evolution of design. It seeks to change future society through the evolution of concepts, relationships, as well as the mould of design. In bringing out the beauty in new forms, it believes that today's designers need to find values that connect with the next generation in new ways.

O Street

Pages 106–109

Based in the UK, O Street is a branding and creative studio that balances process with play to get things right for the good people it works with (while having far too much fun).

Oksana Drachkovska

Born and currently based in Ukraine, Oksana Drachkovska is an illustrator and artist who regularly collaborates with publishing houses, magazines, and design studios on top of working on her own creative projects.

OrtnerSchinko

For OrtnerSchinko, a design studio that works across print and digital mediums, there is no 'either-or' when it comes to strategies for art direction, design, and materials that work. Founded by Kira Saskia Schinko and Wolfgang Ortner in 2015, it constantly looks at reduction to put the essential in the spotlight, and focuses on uniqueness that speaks volumes visually to highlight the value of graphic design.

Passport

Founded by Jonathan Finch and Rosalind Stoughton in 2012, Passport is an independent branding and print design studio based in the UK. It strives to deliver carefully-crafted, well-executed print and digital resolutions as a result of constant research and experimentation with unconventional processes and materials.

Power-nap Over Design Studio

Power-nap Over is a Hong-Kong based design studio that was founded by Vita Mak in 2013. It strives to introduce timeless products and an influential lifestyle through projects that revolve around art direction, branding, and the like. Vita believes that design can be a tool of social change or, at the very least, a powerful means to influence people's ways of living.

Studio Riebenbauer

With a strong belief in never walking beaten paths, and carving new ones to craft memorable and unique brands instead, Vienna-based Studio Riebenbauer is all about creating deep experiences by breaking genres and limits. As one of the few one-stop shops in Europe, they focus on expressing all aspects of a brand, from classic communication and design work to branded spaces and architecture.

Studio Simone Post

Dutch textile and product designer Simone Post's work is characterised by material experiments, in-depth research, as well as a love for colour, print, and crafts.

Tamara Kostianovsky

Tamara Kostianovsky is a Latin artist whose work addresses important themes such as the environment, violence, and consumer culture; often employing discarded clothing to create visceral and intricate sculptures and installations. Her award-winning work has been exhibited at various notable venues around the world. A Guggenheim Fellowship, New York Foundation for the Arts, and Pollock-Krasner Foundation grant recipient, she holds a BFA from the National School of Fine Arts in Buenos Aires, and an MFA from the Pennsylvania Academy of the Fine Arts in Philadelphia.

Yorgo&Co
Pages 110-113

Founded by award-winning designer Yorgo
Tloupas and Emmanuelle Beaudet, Yorgo&-
Co is a multidisciplinary design studio based
in Paris. Since 1996, Yorgo has been involved
in various international branding and identity
design projects while working as a renowned
art director for a large number of magazines.
Besides teaching at Penninghen in Paris and
ECAL in Lausanne, he has also given speeches
and hosted workshops worldwide.

Zoo Studio
Pages 048-049

Barcelona-based Zoo Studio focuses on
working to extremely high standards with the
aim of constantly surpassing expectations. Its
team is made up of people from different yet
complementary educational and professional backgrounds to ensure effective creative
outcomes.

Zunder OG
Pages 020-023

With no fear of the extraordinary, Zunder is an
Austrian design studio that is powered by joy.
Rather than search for the right answer, it is all
about emotional impact and passion.

ACKNOWLEDGEMENTS

We would like to specially thank all the designers and
studios who are featured in this book for their significant
contribution towards its compilation. We would also like to
express our deepest gratitude to our producers for their
invaluable advice and assistance throughout this project,
as well as the many professionals in the creative industry
who were generous with their insights, feedback, and time.
To those whose input was not specifically credited
or mentioned here, we truly appreciate your support.

FUTURE EDITIONS

If you wish to participate in viction:ary's future projects
and publications, please send your portfolio to:
submit@victionary.com